Written and Created by
Luis Mustillo

STEELE SPRING
STAGE RIGHTS

www.stagerights.com

Steele Spring Stage Rights
3845 Cazador Street
Los Angeles, CA 90065
(323) 739-0413

www.stagerights.com

CHARACTERS

Bobby – Bartender for 32 yrs. Knows the trade inside and out. Smart. In command. Tough, but not an asshole. Good guy who doesn't fuck around. Like in the script, he's giving this kid a shot. It's 9:30am midtown, upscale establishment.

Richard – Good hearted, sweet guy. If he didn't bartend he would be a writer or an artist. He is a bartender though and he's quite fine with that. Loves New York more than anyone. He's a good friend. Will do anything for you. Smart with his money but not cheap. He's a romantic. He does not feel sorry for himself, even when he's sad. It's Christmas Eve and he's tipsy, but not drunk. It's 3am, 8th Ave saloon.

Patty – NUTS, FUN, ODD. LOUD. Great bartender. Proud of his standing as a lifer bartender. Likes to get stoned, but far from your hippie, stoner type. Finds Joe Friday, hotdogs, broads and tips all fascinating. It's after his shift. 3rd Ave. (Works at Smith & Woliensky Grill, 49th & 3rd Ave, Mon– Thurs 7pm– 2am.)

Benny – Old Time Queens bartender. Works at a corner saloon since 1977. Before that, another corner saloon. Twice divorced, gambler, drinker. Money problems. All he knows is bartending. 3:45am Astoria, Queens.

Jimmy – One time high rolling bar owner. Been in the business all his life. Lost it all to drugs. He's HIV positive, not on death's door, but also not a vision of health. He's a survivor. He wants to live. He has not given up.

Eddie – Slight lisp. Lazy tongue they call it. Looks like Haus Cartwright. Uses his arms and hands as punctuation. He's fun. He's honest. He is classic.

** This play can be done with one, two, three or six actors.

PLACE & TIME
Bars throughout New York city and state, present day.

SETTING
Stage needs a Bar 6 to 7 feet long, 3 bar stools, a table and a chair. The bar sits stage right on an angle. The table, stage and chair stage left. Some audiences will see the back of the bar. That would be up to the set designer. Whatever works to make it look real.

Lights can adjust to director's notion of the time and place. Music of the directors choice can be used between pieces during black outs.

COSTUME & PROPS
Costumes: Black pants, white shirt, bar apron for "Training"
Rain coat for "Christmas on 8th Avenue"
Black vest for "4am That's What I'm Worth"
Beat up sport coat for "Knee deep in the Hudson"

Props: Bar Rag, liquor bottles, stir sticks, Coffee Cup, 2 Rocks glasses.

RUNNING TIME
1 Hour 15 Minutes

AUTHOR'S NOTE

I wrote the show for my father who was a life-long bartender in Buffalo, New Yrok. He worked behind the stick for fifty-four years and was working (semi-retired) two days a week when he passed away. He was the most street wise guy I ever met... and that's saying something. I wish him well and I miss him. He was what one would call a stand up guy. He could connect with a cross section of people on a level that amazed me. He taught me how to bartend and it served me well. The play consists of six different bartenders and it's about me Dad and the many characters I have come across over the years while serving drunks. I bartended until I was thirty-one years of age and I could do it now if need be. BARTENDERS received Best Solo Play nominations from the LA Weekly Theater Awards in Los Angeles and The Outer Circle Critics in New York City. It was also translated to Danish and had a long run in Copenhagen.

BOBBY – TRAINING

BOBBY

I called you in early to re-train you– go through everything all over again. Just like it's day one. Because you've been here two weeks and it's not working out. And, I don't like training people. I figure if you don't know how to bartend at this point you're fucked anyway. So I'm giving you a shot here. You have bartended before right?… So do you know what you're doing?… You're not one of those fuckers from those bartending schools are ya?… Good… because I can't stand those people.

So you know what's going on?… Good… Ok, the register is simple… hit vodka, gin, etcetera. Call, top shelf. Domestic beer, imported beer, etcetera. You just don't hit any key you feel like. Press total to cash the check out, press tab to keep it running. Simple. We'll go through it again once we open. We got a few minutes… Now, you should know all the regulars in a few days. Everyone else that wants to run a tab, they gotta give you a credit card. I don't care what any of 'em say to you. That's your responsibility. When you come in at six, you have to order whatever beers you're low on. The bus boy will bring them out to you– *you* gotta stock them. There's always fruit in the back cooler. If not, you'll have to cut some. Hardly ever though, because I do it during the day.

At night– at closing– all the bottles in the speedracks and on the shelves get wiped down and locked up in the cabinets. They want them locked up now because the cleaning crew was drinking booze all morning for weeks on end. They couldn't figure out why the liquor cost was so high. They were putting the pressure on everybody. One morning, five a.m., the manager stops in and three guys are sitting here drinking Cordon Blue. Fucking Cordon Blue… out of the bottle. They got fired, but now we gotta lock up all the shit just in case.

Also the speedracks get wiped down– all of them. The bar gets wiped down of course. You put away all the fruit and everything, lock up all the coolers and cabinets. Those cleaning guys made our job harder. But that's the way it is. If you ever fill in days, you set up everything just like I do. There are no more ashtrays. So you just put up the bowls of pretzels or whatever shit they got. When you work days, you have to stock all the juices, stock all the beer, make the sweet and sour mix, which I'll show you, and you have to cut all the fruit. During the day a lot more people eat lunch at the bar now because you can't smoke at the bar. You can't smoke at any bar in the world now. I can't get used to this. You can't smoke in France now. You what that's like in France? That's like telling an American they gotta go outside to eat a cheeseburger. It's fucking ridiculous. Everyone likes it… I don't… but that's the way it is… Okay, you'll work service today and tonight at happy hour. That means you have all the waiters and waitresses… plus…

He gestures towards the end of the bar where costumers would be sitting. He does not get an answer so he continues teaching

BOBBY (CONT'D)

...the customers at this end of the bar. Get the bar customers first. I'll repeat that... *get-the-bar-customers-first.* Because the wait staff doesn't tip. It's been like that since the fuckin' fifties. In the 30 years I've been here, I've tried numerous times to change that. They won't do it. So *fuck them.* Let 'em wait. Get the people who tip first– the customers. Then get them after. You're new, they'll all bitch. Just let them. Also, as you know...

He looks around to see if anyone from management is in the house yet. It's clear. He motions to the rookie to sit at the table. Gets a cup of coffee from behind the bar.

...sit down...

He crosses and sits at the table facing the audience. Note: we must believe that the rookie is sitting in the chair opposite him.

...as you know, a corporation owns this place. If it were run the way they wanted, the place would be empty. Like, what they expect their liquor cost should be is unheard of. They expect it to be at 18. Most places buy the staff dinner if it gets below 20. Here they *expect* it to be at 18. It's impossible. They know it. They just say that so no one will buy anyone a drink. Of course, you have to buy the regulars a couple of rounds a night. You have to– this is New York, not Kansas or Los Angeles or Phoenix or wherever. This is... New York. You have to, or you'll lose them, there's too many places. So how we get around that, is we do little things that add up.

Like at the service bar, whenever a waiter or waitress orders a pina colada type deal or a daiquiris– any of that pain in the ass shit– you never pour in a full shot of booze. Just keep the blender blending. Add water– then just top it off. So their first sip they taste booze. Just a touch. No one orders those drinks except people on vacation or people sitting at tables because they're not really drinkers and they're not really drinks. Anyone who's not in Hawaii and orders a pina colada type drink is not a drinker. So basically, you're doing them a favor. They'll all feel much better in the morning when they're at the... zoo or The Seaport or whatever the fuck they do. Also any drink like Stoli and grapefruit at the service bar– just pour in well vodka. Never in a million years is the person gonna know it's not Stoli. That's the stupidest thing in the world anyway. Ruining a good vodka like that. This Kettle One and coke bullshit. So in my mind, I have no problem with that.

See, people drink what they think they're drinking– unless it's a hard core Scotch on the rocks guy or a hard core bourbon on the rocks guy. People drink what they think they're drinking. It's all up here. It's all psychological. Always has been. During the sixties, seventies and eighties this place was *the* spot to get whiskey sours. Everyone came here for the whiskey sours.

BOBBY (CONT'D)

Best in Manhattan. Because why– we make 'em from scratch. Sweet and sour mix we make ourselves– add powdered sugar, shake well, foam– cherry– the best– 1965 to1985.

My first day here I made maybe twelve of them. All through lunch. Then at five, the night guy comes in– old vet. Anal guy. Angry. Pain in the ass. Gets his checks together, says hello, etcetera. All of a sudden he looks down at me and says, "What the fuck are you doing?" I say, "I'm making a whiskey sour." As I'm putting in the powdered sugar– he says "Are you crazy?" I say "What?" He takes me off to the side and tells me that I'm putting in dish-washing soap. I had been putting in white dish washing soap, all day, instead of the powdered sugar. They foamed up beautiful, perfect, all day. Moral of the story– not one of them got sent back. Why? Because this is where you get the best whiskey sour in town... get it... OK...

Another thing– we get a lot of foreigners in here as you know during happy hour when it's busy. I don't know why they like the place, but they do. Always in big groups, always on an expense account credit card with some company name on it. They stay for hours. They drink a lot. The thing is– they never ever, ever tip. Check could be $300, they got you running your ass of– not a dime– consistently. So... how we help ourselves out and even things up... is after everyone's drunk, we buy the regulars rounds throughout the evening... and we put them on the foreigners' check... I'd be telling you this in a week, I might as well tell you now. I'm not going to waste my time with this stuff anymore. I'm too old. We all do it, we have to. There's a million things going on, they don't know, they got a hundred drinks on their check, they don't look, they don't care, some company's paying for it. So now the big tippers are being treated well and they tip bigger. The foreigners, who don't tip, buy the big tippers drinks, we don't fuck with the liquor cost and it all works out...

Now, if the foreigners ever do start tipping– we stop doing it. I mean, I'm not a scumbag. None of us are. But somehow, *somehow*... they gotta come up. They gotta come up. You can't just come in here all the time, stay for hours, take up half the bar and never tip. You just can't. You just can not. Can't do it. We work for tips, that's how we live, ring up a lot of booze for the company and make tips. There's no other reason to be here. Good service, clean service, fast service– tips. That's it.

That's why anytime someone doesn't tip on a round– you gotta keep track. This is not when they're sitting at the bar, this is when they pick the drinks up and walk away. When it's busy and they gotta stand over by the windows or wherever. They get their third round and still no tip– unless they're running a tab of course– I'm talking cash for rounds– three rounds, no tip– you point the guy out to me or whoever you're working with. That customer now– after three rounds becomes... invisible.

BOBBY (CONT'D)

He walks up again– you look right through him, around him, over him. You serve everyone around him, except him. If there's no one else to serve, you just stand there still not hearing him or seeing him. I don't care if he pleads, begs, cries, weeps, blows off a fucking flare gun– you walk away, wash glasses, whatever.

Now, I know what you're thinking– maybe he's going to tip at the end. Right? Bullshit. He don't even *know* he's getting another round each time he orders. He's just not tipping. So, then after a fair enough amount of time you approach the guy like it's the first time you ever saw him and quietly mention that we work for tips. Then take his order. Dollars to donuts, he'll come up good to save face. Or in some cases, he'll say fuck you and leave, which is fine too. Who needs him. If he ever goes to the manager, which they hardly ever do– you just deny you ever saw him.

OK– last thing– they have spotters here. You know what a spotter is right? They're like narcs. They act like customers and they watch us for the company. They make reports. The thing is, they're easy to spot– so to speak. They don't drink. They'll order soda water and nurse it for hours and they don't talk to people. You can ask them if they're a spotter and if they are they have to say yes. It's the law. I found this out. I do it every few years. You don't want to do that a lot cause you look guilty. So if you feel it in your bones, you have an instinct about a guy– just behave. By the book. Ring up every drink the minute you make it. Because they don't understand a good bartender can keep track in his head– while he's making another round for someone else. That he can do both at once. They just think you're not ringing the one drink up. So be slow– and do it. You'll get the feel as to what they look like after a while. They look like... assholes. They look like those moral majority fuckers you see on TV. They look like they don't like bars. So just keep an eye out... OK?... That's it... This place is a pain in the ass basically. I wouldn't wish it on my worst enemy and I've been here a long time. But the money's good. It's steady, it's busy and it's good. The most important thing about being a good bartender is that you're a stand up guy, is that you're loyal to your fellow bartenders... Okay?... So be nice and be clean and be fast and we'll do fine. Alright... let me finish this–

Gestures to coffee.

–we'll go back there, have some fun.

END SCENE

<u>RICHARD – CHRISTMAS ON 8TH AVENUE</u>

RICHARD

Here we are Stevie, Christmas Eve on 8th Avenue.
(singing, doing a few mick jagger moves)
I can't give it away on 8th Avenue, this town is where it tatters, sha do bee, my brains are battered, splattered all over Manhattan.
(speaking)
Were you busy tonight, man? We rock and rolled. All the people getting drunk before going off to their planes and trains. I made some money.
Crosses down center, looks out the front window.
I also had a few after work as you can see. Stevie, it's snowing out. That's nice, nice effect for the holidays. Christmas. *Christmas! Ho Ho Ho!*
Crosses back.
You know what I hate about Christmas?... I mean it's great when you're a bartender, you make great money... but, other than that... you know what I hate about it? It's a memory day. It's a geiger counter for all the highs and lows. And that's why I don't like it. That's why I'm staying here alone tomorrow... and I'm going to ignore it. 'Cause I'm the *Lone* Ranger. I'm a man without romance. I envy you, man. Tomorrow morning you take the train to meet the woman you love on Christmas. I know that well. And all I can say is– God bless you, Steven. You're a fortunate man. Because it's lovely. It's truly nice... You want to hear my favorite Christmas?... You're my close friend Stevie, I've never told anyone this. My all time favorite Christmas...
The story begins.
OK... a few years ago my old girlfriend and me stayed here in the city for Christmas– and I've never been here on Christmas *day* before. I always split late Christmas Eve or early Christmas morning. So I was excited, I couldn't wait! I had it all planned out! Christmas Eve we went out all afternoon, The Algonquin, The St. Regis, PJ Clarks, we strolled in Central Park, food, drinks. Then! We went down to Little Italy, and it was all lit up, but by 8-9 o'clock a lot of the places were closed. Now this was new to me. I never knew it closed down so much. It was like a small town. I kinda dug it.

So we walked to the Village and it was real quiet and the snow was falling and all the decorations and there was nobody out on the street... And we came upon Villa Misconi Restaurant on MacDougal Street. Stevie, the place was packed! It was like every New Yorker was in there, having Christmas Eve dinner... And Sinatra singing "Silver Bells," and they had this nice little tree, everybody at the bar was buying drinks, saying Merry Christmas. We sat down, had this great dinner, everyone had a smile on their face! It was wonderful!

RICHARD (CONT'D)

Then... after dinner, on the way home,... we got a tree. And I'm tellin ya Stevie, this is the night to get a tree. Christmas Eve! Cause, those guys know they can't sell anymore, it's over, the stuff's mulch. They're just hanging out. So I walk up to this guy and I point to this tree and say "How much?" He says "$35" I say, "How 'bout $10." He says, "$10's good."... So we drag the tree home, her and me dragging it, laughing. We got home, put on Nat King Cole, had a glass of wine, decorated the tree, made love and fell asleep. Perfect day. The next day, Christmas, we got up early and turned on the Yule log... Stevie, the Yule Log... on Channel 11. It's back! Where you been? The Yule Log, for all the 8 million people without fireplaces. So we watched that and exchanged gifts and hung around. Then we walked down 5th Avenue and it was pretty empty except for around St. Patrick's but you could hear the Allelujah echoing.

(singing some Handel's messiah)

"HALLELUJAH, HALLELUJAH, HALLELUJAH, HALLELUJAH, HALLELUJAH..."

(speaking)

You could hear it out on the street. It was gorgeous. Then we walked to Rockefeller Center sat and drank beer out of deli cups and watched the skaters, with the tree and the music... and before you know it, the sun was going down and we were getting' kinda hungry, but not much was open, so we went home turned on the lights and the tree, and we did something I've always wanted to do my whole life on Christmas... We ordered Chinese food. Stevie... Chinese food on Christmas– in New York City! The place I love more than anywhere else in the world! And the lights were blinking and Jimmy Stewart was on and I remember the place looked great. It was the combination of the glow of the TV with the lights and the tree. Plus, the brownstones across the street were all lit up. The snow was falling. We got under this big quilt, watched Jimmy Stewart. And ate Chinese food.

(pause)

How bout that? That's my all time favorite Christmas.

(pause)

Tell me how can you spend a Christmas like that with someone and then never know them again? How does that happen? It happens a lot I guess. See that's the mother fucker. This time of year. All this shit comes up. I don't think of this shit any other time. Now I see people in the bar, in love, happy, it bugs me.

So get this... the other night I'm working, and this guy I kind of know and his wife stop in. They were on their way home but they decided to stop for a drink. So I got 'em a drink and we're talking– and this guy's kind of an idiot– and at one point he mentions that my ex got engaged last month... Yeah... he just says it, like he was on a mission... And I'm thinking, "Well I know what she's doing for Christmas." And then I started thinking "Boy... that was fast. That was just a little too fast." You know, I'm standing there trying to look casual.

RICHARD (CONT'D)

My stomach was in my shoes. And I'm trying to act normal. They finally got up, said Merry Christmas and left.

After work I walked home from 68th street, 80 below and I didn't feel a thing. I was just walking. And every time I saw a Chinese restaurant, and you see a lot of 'em walking down from 68th street, I started thinking about... you know... the whole thing, you know, that mechanism, that trigger... And I felt this sadness, this anger, this why-is-it-worth-it feeling. You know... all that time, all that love, all the closeness, all the effort, all the madness and they replace you and you replace them and it all starts all over again. I never quite grasp that. I don't think any of us do... And you know the real reason we split up?... She said I had no dreams. She'd deny this, but it's true. She said I had no desire to be anything, except a bartender. And I said, "Well, I like it. It's my chosen profession." But she said "No, it's not a profession, it's a job." And I said "Oh no, you're wrong there sweetheart." You can tell a pro from an amateur a mile away...

No it's definitely a profession. It's a classic profession. It's a noble profession. You have to be everybody in one day to total strangers and there's booze involved. You have to make everyone feel at home. You have to be welcoming and attentive and fast and in control and *smart*, contrary to what people think. No, working in a toll-booth, that's a job. Anyone can do that. But not anyone can be a good bartender. That's what I said. I was offended. But, she said she couldn't see us together years from now and me still doing what I'm doing. She needed more, obviously. She hated the fact that I was content with being what I am. Stevie... I'm a bartender... I don't understand that. I don't get it... Because I did nothing to—

> He thinks "deserve it." But does not say it.
>
>   *(pause)*

You know, I've been putting money away for years, Stevie... years. I don't tell anyone this. I started from day one, getting it out of my hands, that quick cash and putting it in places I can't touch till I get older. Over twenty years I've been doing this. I buy everything cash, I don't owe anyone a nickel. Zero debt. Because this work is steady. Someone always wants a drink. And I show up and I work hard, and I keep socking it away and socking it away and socking it away. I know I'm in better shape than a lot of the suit and tie guys I serve everyday. Guys who are hocked up to their ass.

> *(as if serving the suits)*

"Yes sir," "No sir," "How are you today, sir?"– people she always saw as successful– and I laugh to myself. We went out. We went on trips. We did anything we wanted to do. I talked to her about anything she needed to talk about. I was honest. I was loyal. I was attentive.

RICHARD (CONT'D)

I was right *there*... but, in the end, all she saw... truly... was that... I'm a bartender. None of that other stuff mattered... and that's a shame. That's such a shame.
(pause)
And, why did I even have to hear that? I could have missed those people Stevie... 10 minutes and I was gone. But, no, I had to hear it. See, that's the curse of the bartender. Once you're back there, you always have to hear *everything*. I don't mind being miserable on my own terms, now I have to be miserable on her terms– her decisions. And you know, it was out of my system. I'm tellin' you. I was feeling good. Then these two assholes gotta stop in and all of this holiday bullshit comes along. I hear that and I'm confused. I'm questioning myself. I feel guilty. And why? For what? Because I do what I do? Because it's Christmas? The special time of the year? Well I don't think the joy is going to hit me any time soon... this year at least... But, boy... I would give anything for another one of those Chinese food Christmases... That was fun... that was really fun.
                    Crosses to window again.
It's still snowing. I like it when it snows.
                    (pause)
Alright man, I'm gonna let you go,– no, no, no, you gotta get up early tomorrow. No, I gotta go...

> *He gestures to imaginary money he has left on the bar. Actor must make believe there is money there.*

Take it. Take it. Stevie, take that money, Stevie– take-the-money-off-the-bar. Ah, Jesus Christ, what are you goofy? It's Christmas for Christ's sake, *take* it... Alright, now you have a *wonderful, great* time tomorrow Stevie, give everyone a hug for me. I'll be in my pad tomorrow figuring out what pills I'm going to use for the big exit...

> *Stevie warns him on the stupidity of that though.*

Nooo... come on, I'm fuckin around. Never *that* bad. I'll be back to work the 26th. Workin', keeping my mind off everything, it'll be great. Until then
                    (singing)
"IT'S A QUARTER TO THREE,
THERE'S NO ONE IN THE PLACE
EXCEPT YOU AND ME,

SO SET UP STEVIE,
I GOT A LITTLE STORY
I THINK YOU SHOULD KNOW,

IT'S CHRISTMAS MY FRIEND,
AND I'M ALONE
FOR THIS BRIEF EPISODE,

RICHARD (CONT'D)
(singing)
SO GIVE ME ONE FOR MY BABY,
AND ONE MORE FOR THE ROAD.

THE LONG, SO LONG, THE LONG."
Exit.

<u>END SCENE</u>

PATTY – JOE FRIDAY

PATTY

I'm a lifer– that's fine with me. Come in, walk to work, work my shift, make good money– fuck it. I owned my own joint once, pain in the ass. Plus, this is when the coke thing was running rampant. The 80s– Fucking insane my man… everybody looked like they were eating powdered donuts. Myself included. I had a problem. Not a big problem but enough of a problem. So, I cleaned up my act, came to New York, didn't know many people– by good fortune landed what I consider the best bartending gig in the city. A well-lit businessman's bar.

Fuck it. Hard drinkers, big tippers– no politically correct assholes. Just hard boozing, cigar smoking, no-nonsense saloon men. Hard working, drinkers. You make sure you know them by name, you make 'em feel special, roll out the red carpet. They walk in with a broad and you really treat 'em nice. "Hey Roger– how are you my man– good to see ya. And hello to the lovely lady. Good guy ya got here sweetheart. Oh I hear an accent, where ya from?– Paris Texas. Little flat there isn't it? Isn't that the only place in the country where you can sit on your front porch and watch your dog run away for three days?" The girl's all like "Ooh, Roger knows the bartender– how Daymon Runyon– I must be in the New York." Roger loves it, the girl's impressed, two drinks, leaves me a twenty. "Thank you, Roger. Nice to meet you dear, see you again soon." The wacked-out bartender, they throw money at ya. Throw it at ya. Oh, I get ten of them a night, my man– "Pat, this is Gwenyth." "Gwenyth, lovely to see you– keep an eye on this guy. Ha-Ha-Ha!"– twenty– "Hey, how you two doing, you going to Vegas tonight– tie the knot? Ha-Ha-Ha!"– Twenty. "Hey, nice outfit, he buy it for you? Ha-Ha-Ha!" Twenty. Like a violin, my man, like a well-tuned violin. The money's fantastic.

Me and my girlfriend, we live good. Nice apartment, a block away, walk to work. I got no complaints. No complaints whatsoever. Saturday's and Sunday's my nights off. Nice dinners, get outta town. Florida a couple weeks a year. Golf. See, that's fine with me. I like the job. I'm a bartender, that's what I do. I'm not a singer, I'm not an actor, I'm not a poet. I'm not back there moping around goin', "Oh, I'm not really a bartender, this is just what I do to pay my bills." No. I am a bartender and I'm a good one. Fuckin' proud of it. It's a lost art form. I'm happy back there. I'm at home. When it's slow, I'm not back there reading a magazine. I talk to people, tell stories, fuck around, laugh.

Like people always ask me to tell certain stories. Like the Dragnet story. "Tell the Dragnet story Patty!" They yell it out… Oh I'll tell ya, my man, it's classic… Years ago my mother would send me these hot dogs from upstate. Sahlen Hot Dogs. Best fucking hot dog in the world bar none.

Once you try 'em you're converted for life. I don't care if you're a vegetarian, it's over. But they gotta be char-broiled. So I'm trying everything.

PATTY (CONT'D)

I'm frying 'em, I'm baking 'em, I'm boiling 'em, I'm holding 'em over the open flame, like a fool. I'm putting 'em in the broiler. Nothing's working. They taste mediocre. And I love these hotdogs. So, I go out on my fire escape, small habachi, lotta smoke,the guy above me calls the cops. So I'm fucked. I got these great hotdogs in the freezer, I'm dying to eat em' and I'm fucked. So I come home one night after work, sit down, relax, smoke a joint... tune into my 3 a.m. nightly Dragnet episode on TV Land. Love Dragnet my man!!! Fuckin' Joe Friday kills me!

> *He does a good Joe Friday voice. He also walks like him while he speaks.*

"Just the facts, ma'am." "You're under arrest punk."
> *(back to his own voice)*

You know? Right? He's fuckin' nuts, that guy. With the hairdo, and the suit. He's too much! And I've seen almost every one of them, like my favorite is the one about the guy who does acid and paints his face blue. Did you ever see that one?... Oh, my man, fuckin great... the guy does acid and paints his face blue!

> *(does a voice of a guy on acid— whatever that might be to you)*

"I'm trippin', I painted my face blue. I'm trippin my balls off, my face is painted blue. I'm the blue boy."
> *(back to his own voice)*

Joe Friday sayin,
> *(Joe Friday voice)*

"You shouldn't do acid, you little freak."
> *(back to his own voice)*

Oh, I get stoned, and laugh my ass off! They're classic... So that night the episodes about—
> *(Joe Friday voice)*

"Every now and then a cop needs a day off"
> *(back to his own voice)*

Joe says. And it's all about Joe Friday and Bill Gannan got dates over at Joe's pad... And I never seen them with broads before! I've never seen this episode. I didn't know what their situation was. They're drinking martinis! They lock their guns in the drawer before they start drinking!

> *He mimes them taking their guns out of their under the sportcoat holsters and putting them in a drawer. He then says "ok" in official cop voice as if to say both men admire what they have done in the name of safety.*

"OK?" "OK."

PATTY (CONT'D)
(back to his own voice)

...And Bill Gannan's girl is late and they're waiting for her. That's the whole episode.

(as Joe Friday)

"Is she coming?"

(as Bill Gannon)

"I don't know."

(as Joe Friday)

"You want another drink?"

(as Bill Gannon)

"OK."

(back to his own voice)

Fuckin' Dragnet! So middle of the show Joe says,

(as Joe Friday)

"Well, let me start on the burgers"

(back to his own voice)

...He walks over and slides this grill into his fireplace!

> *HE IS STILL AMAZED BY THIS AND WILL BE*
> *FOR THE REST OF HIS LIFE.*

Now *I* gotta fireplace my man. Nice one, works. I'm sitting there stoned out of mind going "no way... *no way.*" I'm thinking about the hot dogs. I'm all excited. I can't wait to get up the next morning. I look in the yellow pages. I call the Third Avenue Grill Store. "How ya doin'? Look I was stoned out of my mind last night watching Dragnet and Joe Friday sticks this grill into his fireplace— is that just crazy Dragnet shit, or do these things exist?" Girl says "Fireplace grills. We got all kinds." "I'll be right down" I say! Fuckin' *beautiful,* my man!!! The education of Dragnet at 3am. Now I got the hotdogs going like Joe Friday.

(Joe Friday voice)

"How ya doin'? You want a martini?"

(back to his own voice)

...The customers go nuts over that story. Joe Friday. Dragnet...

> *He sits in chair center stage.*

See I have fun back there, I talk to people, I like people. I love the women who come in. Love 'em! Well dressed business women. Country club girls. And they *drink*! Love to drink! I always say free drinks for anyone with a black bra on. We all laugh. They show me the straps on their bra. "I gotta black one Patty." "Here you go dear— Chardonnay on me." And we all laugh... I had to stop doing that though. Some broad complained to the manager. Yeah, she complained to Billy the manager. Never been in the place. First time. Walks in off the street,

PATTY (CONT'D)
(does pain in ass woman voice– whatever that may be to you.)
"Excuse me, *excuse me*, I don't appreciate that. That bra thing, that's offensive."
(back to his own voice)
…Everybody at the bar's going…

> HE leans away from the imaginary woman the way barflies might to distance themselves from a pain in the ass.

Ah, be a sport, you know.

> HE leans in and speaks to the imaginary woman

"Excuse me, sweetheart… I don't know if you've noticed… It's a bar!… *It's a bar*!.. If you can't take it, stay home in the cocoon… watch The View– I don't know– It's a bar."
(he's back to speaking to his friend)
Some people are so fuckin' serious nowadays. Prudes. They're still drinking though. That's for sure. Some of them might have lost their sense of humor, but they're all still drinking. Which is fine with me. Absolutely fine with me– keep *drinking*! That's what I say– What time is it, uh oh? Quarter to three– uh oh–
(Joe Friday voice, Joe Friday walk toward his friend)
"You're under arrest punk."
HE laughs.
(back to own voice)
Alright my man, nice talking to you as always– all the best– get home safe– see ya tomorrow night.
EXIT.

END SCENE

BENNY – 4 A.M. THAT'S WHAT I'M WORTH

BENNY

It's unbelievable… the whole thing…

> *HE looks toward the window. Someone wants in for a drink but the door is locked and BENNY is closed.*

…We're closed… We're done… We're– This fuckin' guy. We're *done*…

> *HE reaches under the bar to turn off the sign in the window. Lighting change takes place as if a lighted sign turned off. The man looking for drink leaves and BENNY continues the story to his friend, Donny.*

No, I could've sued people plenty of times in my life. But I don't think that way. Stupid. One time I'm on Continental Airlines to Vegas. I'm hung-over, so I go to the back of the plane. The flight was empty. So I go take a whole row for myself to relax. I'm jittery– I don't like to fly. I know deep down I shouldn't be going to Vegas. I'm going through a divorce. I'm on edge. So I order a Stoli on the rocks, right? I need to loosen up. So I'm sitting there drinking my drink, minding my own business, relaxing… all of a sudden, outta the blue, Donny, I get this hot flash like I think I'm gonna die. Like..

> *HE does a version of himself reacting to the hot-flash.*

Wow! Like my head's gonna explode. I'm sweating and shaking. I don't know what the fuck is going on. I drink more Stoli to cool off, right? Ten minutes later– again– *Jesus Christ!*

> *Does pain and confusion caused by the hot-flash once again.*

Like battery acid through my whole body. Now I'm thinking my heart is gonna explode. I'm breathing heavy– I drink *more* Stoli. Five minutes later - again.

> *HE does pain and confusion of hot-flash again.*

"*Christ* on the *cross*, what is this?" So I run my hands over my head to regain control…

> *Runs hands over his head. This next section dealing with the coffee can be physicalized by the actor in any way to help him tell the story or not.*

…and I feel this small wet spot. I'm goin' "what the fuck?" So I get up, open up the over-head compartment– I swear to God! There's a pot of *hot coffee*– I swear to God– on a tray, half tipped on its side and there's this small drop comin' out, down the bottom edge of the thing, going along… going along… going along– boom– drip– right on my fuckin' head. I'm thinking all this time it's coming from inside, like I'm gonna die. It's the scalding fucking coffee– a minute scalding drop hitting my head.

BENNY (CONT'D)

So I call the stewardess down– she says "Oh my God, I'm so sorry– I put it up there for a minute to get something and I forgot all about it." I'm thinking "are you kidding me? Are you nuts?" So I say "that's bad, that's really bad." I'm delirious, I'm all fucked up. That's all I say– "That's bad, that's really bad." They buy me a drink and that was it. Like a fucking idiot.

I think about it now, I could own that fucking airline. I could've sued them for millions or at least flown for free for the rest of my life– something. That lady sued McDonalds for five million dollars and she *bought* the coffee. This coffee had nothing to do with me. And I don't say a goddamn thing. I get off the plane and lose a bundle in Vegas. Stupid ass.

Now especially with this guy suing me. I mean what the fuck? Some asshole I don't even know. I can't believe this. I serve drinks. That's what I do for a living. I serve drinks. The guy walks in. Walks in– doesn't stumble. Speaks clearly. No sign of trouble. Orders a bourbon rocks. No problem. He's not swaying, he's not loud, he's not slurring. Nothing. He orders two more. No problem. Now some guys– and you know this– some guys– you can be in this business from *day one*– some guys don't show it when they're drunk. I've seen guys like this my whole life. 50 drinks, they don't change their attitudes, their speech, their posture– nothin'. So how the fuck do I know this guy's gonna go out, run into some truck, smash up his caddy and get arrested? That's my fault? The bar's fault? What about the ten drinks he had somewhere else...

Look, I'm sorry it happened, but there are reasons to sue people, like the coffee thing, stupid as I am, but not when a guy orders more drinks when he knows he's driving and then blames the bartender. That's like me taking the coffee and pouring it over my head, and saying "Ahhh... see it shouldn't have been up there." You see what I'm saying?

But, the bottom line is if this thing happens and I get fired, no one in the world is gonna hire me. I might get a night every now and then at a catering hall. Friggin' weddings! I hate working weddings. They give me the skeeves. No one tips, all the in-laws hate each other, but they act friendly. You know the couple's gonna get divorced. It reminds me of my wedding. I hate 'em. They depress me. I can't do it. Without this gig I'd have to leave town. The fuck am I gonna go? I got friends here– family. I mean thank God the guy's OK. All he did was bang his head and smash the car up. Thank God. Then I'd really be screwed– he's dead or whatever. But again, how is it my fault? What the fuck kind of world do we live in? Twenty years ago they'd laugh at this.
        (as a man asking a question 20 years ago)
"Wait, wait, you're telling me some guy gets drunk then *sues* the bartender? Get the fuck outta here. Are you nuts?"

BENNY (CONT'D)
(Benny once again)

Now I'm nervous at work. I'm cutting people off who are stone sober just because they drop something. I'm on edge. I hate it. Thank God Joey let me stay on until we see what happens. Thank God. He's loyal at least.

Shit, I've been with him since 1985. He knows that I'm his guy. But I know if this thing hits, he's got no choice, I know it, I'm gone. And I need the job, Donny... I need the job. I got no money. I got *no* money. Between the divorce and you know... I've had a bad stretch. I owe people. I mean, I'm on such a losing streak I can't function. You know how neurotic and insane I get. Everything has a meaning.

Last time I won, I called the bookie from this one chair, so now, every time I call, I call from this one chair... weeks go by– nothing. Fucking chair turned on me– bad chair. So I move to a different chair, same thing. Bad chair. I stand in the corner to call. I stand in the kitchen. I call from the hallway. Maybe it's the fucking phone? I'm running out of places to call from. I'm running out of places to sit. I don't have a chair I can sit in that I don't think is fuckin' me up somehow. The friggin Kentucky Derby. 9,000 horses running– I pick four I like– last minute I throw two out. Now I got these two horses– I bet them big. Who wins? The horse I threw out! 30 to 1. Now why the fuck I don't do a four horse triple box– cost me $48 dollars– the thing pays seventy five hundred. The superfecta pays,

Donny knows.

right, right... twenty four grand! I *had* the horses. I had them *all!* We go out after the race, Bobby picks up my racing form, says "you got four horses circled– all four of 'em came in– one, two, three, four– what the fuck is wrong with you?" I said "I threw two out." He says "You threw two out? Lotta horses running. You gonna bet– bet." And he's right. He's fucking right. You gonna bet– bet. Fifty more dollars, I walk away with seventy five hundred. I got bills backed up. My rent is killing me. I got this fucking nut suing me. I'm day-to-day. Ask me what I'm worth, go ahead, ask me... it's gotta be right now, four o'clock in the morning– what I got is in my pocket. That's it. The next day it's gone. Come in again, same thing, four a.m.– that's what I'm worth... Jesus Christ...

> *Pause while he picks up a glass from a table and walks across the stage to the bar. He walks the way a man walks when he's on his feet 8 hours a day, 5 days a week for 30 years. It does not matter how old the actor playing him is. It should be in his gut and soul.*

Look, I know this isn't the greatest job in the world, I know that, but without it, I'm done. I got nowhere else to go. I don't know how to do nothing else...

(bartender to the end)

You want another one?

Exit.

END SCENE

JIMMY – 12TH AVENUE

JIMMY

You're paying me for this, right?... Um... I don't know... Um... Well I started working behind the wood when I was 17, over on 10th Avenue. Washing glasses, bussing beer bottles. Stocking, cleaning shit like that. I lied about my age. It was no big deal. The place was a dinner place with a hoppin' bar crowd. Then when I was 19 I started bartending. And I liked it. I always have. I stayed there for awhile, then when I was 22, I started working the clubs. This was... 1980. This is also when I first started doing drugs. They were everywhere. Lot of women too. Because the bartender is the safest guy in the place.

A lot of people don't know that. You know where he works, you know his name. He serves you drinks and most importantly he's the safest because of that three foot wide piece of wood between you and him. That wood is freedom. Behind the wood you can say whatever you want. "Hello ladies." "How are you this evening?" "You all look beautiful tonight." "Where you off to later?" "Can I get you another something?" And they enjoy it. They like it. They tell you anything. Explain all. Accept all compliments. They give you a phone number to call them. They laugh, they listen. They'll stay– they want another drink.

You see, that separation... all your insecurities go out the window because of that separation. Now, be on the other side of the bar, walk up to a woman say, "Hello– how are you? You look beautiful tonight– Where are you off to?– Can I get you a drink?"... You're fucked. You don't get the time of day. No response. If any, it's hostile. Reason being– they didn't have that three feet of bar between them and whoever they're talking to. I did. Very unfair, but very true.

I had my own place for awhile. Got some investors– not a lot of money– cheap. Way over on 11th Avenue We stayed five nights a week open till six am, A lot of bar people getting off of work. A lot of people from the clubs. The place was a drug den, basically. Ton of shit. When you do a lot of speed and cocaine, besides fuckin' up your head and your body and getting paranoid, you drink a lot. *A lot*! I was making a huge amount of money.

The only problem, and any high-line dope dealer will tell you this, is that you can't be a user yourself. That's the key to success. Any long time successful barkeeper is usually not a heavy drinker. At least not while he's in his own place. Now you bring coke and speed into the mix and the stakes go even higher. My rent was $1,800 a month. That's ridiculously low. Some apartments were more expensive. But, somehow I wasn't paying the bills. How that is I don't know. It's a blur. I was having fun. Lots of money, lots of friends, lots of women, lot of laughs. It all seemed like innocent fun. It was fun, for awhile. Never innocent, but fun. Then sooner or later, the stuff takes over. And that's all it is.

JIMMY (CONT'D)

It becomes about that and everything else, slowly sails away and you smile all along. Then, of course, it ends.

They padlocked me two and a half years after I opened. Almost to the day... And that was my dream. Everyone has a dream. That was my dream– owning my own place. All of a sudden I couldn't get anyone on the phone. No more clout, no more friends and I was pretty much broke. That's when people really turn on you. It's one thing to never have it. But when you have it and you loose it. They hate you. You're a fool, and they despise a fool... I was also an addict. By this time I had gone from cocaine to heroin to morphine, back to heroin, to methadone, which is the worst, back to heroin... back to morphine and on and on and on. Morphine started as a pain-killer actually, or at least I convinced myself.

I was fucked up one night and got hit over the head. Beat up pretty bad. I don't know where I was– downtown somewhere. But I got beat up pretty bad. I didn't stay in a hospital because I had no money. So my ex-wife– which is a whole 'nother story– she let me stay with her for awhile, in our original apartment– I had nowhere to go and I was in constant pain. At the time a guy I knew from the old days had access to script morphine, and I needed it. That on top of the fact that a junky's a junky, you *need* everything. And you act like a junky– you beg, you lie, you steal, you do what you do. You do drugs. It doesn't matter what drug it is. They're all pain-killers, right? Isn't that what they say. Physical pain. Emotional pain. All that bullshit. One of my old junky friends used to say, "Pain-killers cause a lot of pain," and we would laugh, start talking about all the shit... like Vicodins, that Mid-western drug– they're really evil. You get some forty-two year old housewife– clean as a whistle, doesn't even drink. Slips on some spilled salad dressing in her kitchen– fucks up her back so bad she can't move. Starts on a few Vicodins– next thing you know she's forging checks, sticking up gas stations– "Whatever happen to Mildred?"– "She's in Attica for armed robbery." "Really?" Horrible shit...

My ex?... She threw me out of course. I don't blame her. Since then I've been out on the street off and on. It's been a slow, long fall... or a quick, long fall. I don't even remember half of it. But it's real. I'm sick now. I got the sickness– I've been OK. I don't know for how long though, don't really think about it.

I just do what they tell me to do... I'm also clean now... which is a fuckin' joke really. It makes absolutely no sense. It's like finding out the bomb's gonna drop and goin' out and remodeling your kitchen. It's stupid... stupid timing... But, I've been working one day a week... at this dive bar– mixed crowd– short shift. This guy used to come into my place, I guess, when he was younger. This gay dude. He said I treated him nice. He saw me on the street, remembered me, gave me a job. I didn't even know him back then and he comes through... more than anyone...

JIMMY (CONT'D)

It's a strange world, man, isn't it? The place in on the West Side Highway. I just keep going farther west. If I live another ten years, I'll be knee deep in the Hudson with a bottle of vodka... a floating bar, tourists. It's OK though. As long as I come to work clean– meaning clean clothes– washed.

I can always pull that together. And I can *always* bartend... And I stay where I can. There's a flop house on 23rd and 11th. I stay there a lot– mostly.

Lemme tell you something... you're asking me... This ain't a new story. There's always gonna be people who fall through. And some survive and some don't. I hope I do. But, I always go back to what I loved most. Back when I was 19, with my bow tie and white shirt. I was making drinks, meeting people. How simple it was. How much fun it was. Having a drink after work. Walkin' home with the sun comin' up, sober, with a woman. Grabbing a cup of coffee. Taking the Staten Island ferry at dawn... I loved that. I think now how happy I'd be just working five nights a week at some corner saloon, with regulars... watching football. Stupid shit. Take a woman to a movie on my night off. Go to dinner... nice glass of wine... some money in my pocket. Take a vacation... That would be nice– a vacation... I haven't had one of those in awhile.

Exit.

END SCENE

<u>EDDIE – BUFFALO</u>

EDDIE

Working the bar by myself– that's how I like it. I don't have to pay anybody. The money's mine. I finally own my own place. Take one day a week off. Closed Sunday. No one downtown anyway. Got this nice kid works Saturday nights. I help out if it gets busy. Got an afternoon guy, Mike, six days a week. He's solid. The other five nights is me– solo– makin' money– keeps me outta trouble. Got no wife, no kids. That pressure's off. Gotta nice girl I see on my night off. Perfect.

The only thing that drives me nuts is the repetition. The bar business, a lot of the same things day in and day out. Plus a lot of people know me. So whenever I go out to a different joint to have a quiet drink, escape for a minute, it's all "Hey Eddie, how's it going?" "Get Eddie a drink." "How you doing Eddie?" I wanna hide. People slapping me on the back. Fuckin' guys huggin' me. I don't like being hugged. I don't like it. If I'm with a girl, we hug, show some emotion, show some affection– that's fine. But other than that, I don't like it. Especially if it's someone I don't really know. I'm always like, "What the fuck's this guy huggin me for?" Who am I? Ed McMann? Like I brought him a check or something. Stop hugging me. I don't like it.

But besides that– that repetition– after all the years working for somebody else– finally I'm the boss, I call the shots. The register is mine. Key to a successful bar– get the money– get the cash. I'll buy a round every now and then. Christmas time– "Merry Christmas everybody– drinks on me." Somebody's birthday, "Happy Birthday– Okay." Somebody has a kid– "Bobby had a kid. His 57th kid. Congratulations, Bobby." Other than that, order the drink, pay me the money, that's that. That's how a bar works.

That's what kills me about bars in movies. You got these movies– everything is realistic. The special effects, the lasers, the aliens, the computer generated thing, the makeup– *very* realistic… someone walks into a bar it goes totally out the window. Maybe once in a while it's realistic, but 99 percent of the time, because I'm sitting there thinking, who the fuck owns this place. Like I love this one, this one kills me– the lead guy of the movie walks into some joint– never been there before– goes to the bar orders a "scotch rocks, vodka rocks" whatever, bartender gives him the drink, the guy takes it, looks at it and goes–

He takes drink and walks away from the bar.

–walks away. What the fuck is that about? Where does that happen? Try that later on tonight. Walk into a bar, you never been to, go to the bar, order a drink, take it and walk away. See what happens -Somebody will jump on ya. New York, they'll kill ya… Happens all the time in the movies. I'd love it if one time the bartender would say, "Hey buddy, excuse me, could you come here for a second?

EDDIE (CONT'D)

Look, I know you're the lead guy in the movie and everything and you got a big scene to do, but you still owe me $5.50 for the scotch. Just trying to run a business, nothin personal. Thanks." Guy just walks away like he's on scholarship.

Pierce Brosnan, someone gave him a gift certificate. That James Bond. He must have a tab in every bar in the world. That guy hasn't paid for a drink since 1962. No money ever. *Cheers* was on for like what 14 years– no one ever paid for a drink. Fuckin' "Norm!" That guy's tab must have been like 300,000 dollars. And then there's the big bartender movie, "Cocktail"– You remember that one– I had to see that one. One minute the guy doesn't know what a Kubalibra is, next thing you know he's juggling bottles... He's pouring over his shoulder, behind his head, through his legs, up his ass, like that's what bartending is. He never waits on anybody. Him and the other guy are throwing bottles to each other,

Mimes throwing bottles.

"You got it?"– "OK. I got it." "Got it." "I got it." "Okay."

Stops throwing bottles.

Now you know, sooner or later, the owner is going to come over– "You want to stop throwing the fuckin' bottles please– you're going to kill somebody, miss– take out half the room." And he's juggling. Now, maybe in Disney World that would be cool, I don't know– "hey look honey, the bartender's a juggler"– "Oh my God"– "How do you think he does that?"– "How the fuck should I know? Wow." But, I been to New York enough times to know a New Yorker's gonna be like "Hey Buddy, you wanna stop juggling for a second and get me a fuckin' drink ?– You wanna juggle? Join the Big Apple Circus– I'm *thirsty,* thanks." And the catchphrase kills me– "When he Pours, he Reins"... Get the fuck outta here... "When he Pours, he Reigns"... How about stop juggling, and ring up a fucking drink, that's what I say. Keep the place in business.

See this business is a lot harder than it looks. That's why anytime someone asks me for a free drink, like "Hey I've been here long time, how 'bout buying me a drink"... That's it... That's it, it's over. Ask any good bartender. Once they ask, its over. That guy doesn't get a free drink on the house now, till the end of the earth. A tidal wave could be on its way, *ten minutes*– everyone dead– *he's* still payin'. I'll be ringin' his drink up when the fuckin wave comes through the front door. I'll be getting washed away by the wave still trying to hit the numbers on the register. Fuck him. Free drink. Like I'm not workin' my ass off. Like any good bartender's not working their ass off... Were you ever in an electronics store, some guy walks in "Hey, I buy my stereo equipment here all the time– how about givin' me a TV?" It's a business. The other thing that drives me nuts is when people ask you to top it off. They don't want a full drink, just a little topper.– "Yeah, just a topper, just a little touch, I don't want a full drink." 4 o'clock in the morning, I don't mind, 8 o'clock at night, different story.

EDDIE (CONT'D)

"Yeah, just a little touch." Like I'm Hickory Farms over here– I'm giving away free samples– "Just half a glass of wine, I don't want a full glass"– "okay"– So, I ring it up. They get pissed off. "Hey you didn't have to ring it up, I just asked for a little touch." "Hey buddy, you can't check into the Waldorff for a nap." You either you want a drink or you don't want a drink. I don't serve half drinks...

See, people think bartending's easy– "Oh, it must be fun, like hangin' out, only you're making money." Whattaya kidding me? It's hard, *real* hard. My lower back's always killing me, carrying buckets of ice, cases of beer, cases of booze. My knees. My legs. My feet. *Psychological* damage... forget it. "Eddie, my wife"... "Eddie, my husband"... "Eddie, my job"... "Eddie, my in-laws"... "Eddie, my mother"... "Eddie, my father"... "Eddie, I'm hung-over"... "Eddie, my ass hurts"... "Eddie, I got arrested"... "Eddie, I'm depressed"... "Eddie, I'm getting divorced"... "Eddie, get me a sandwich"... "Eddie, turn the fan on"... "Eddie, turn the fan off"... "Eddie turn the juke box up"... "Eddie turn the juke down"... "Eddie turn the air conditioner up"... "Eddie, turn the air conditioner down"... "Eddie get me another sandwich."... "Eddie, turn the fan back on"... "Eddie, turn the fan back off."... "Eddie, turn it off"... "Turn it on. Turn it down, turn it over, turn it up, turn it in, turn it out...

> Note: say "Eddie" as many times as you want–
> whatever feels right)

Eddie, Eddie, Eddie, Eddie." *Fuck*– just take a vacuum and suck my brain out... The jukebox, I don't mind– once it's up, it stays up. But the other stuff drives me nuts... Speaking of the jukebox, that's the other important thing, the music. Music can make or break a place. Good music keeps people drinking. Gets people going. Gets me going. Like whenever I hear the song "Revolution" by the Beatles, that song gets me going. That beginning–

> Does the beginning guitar of Revolution, then he
> sings.

> (singing)

"SAY YOU WANT A REVOLUTION, WELL YOU KNOW. WE ALL WANT TO CHANGE THE WORLD."

> (speaking)

That's a heavy song. John Lennon. I did the research on that song. What he's saying is, "I'm in on the protest. I'll protest, but I'm not going to go out and hurt anyone." That's when he says, "count me out– in." So he's saying he's in as far as doing it the way he wants to, which is the peaceful way, but he's out if it gets violent. So what he does instead, he goes and gets wife Yoko Ono... and they stay in bed for a week! Remember that one? I love that one! That was beautiful. Like if everyone just stays in bed for a week, all the soldiers, all the governments, all the dictators, all the armies, all the religions– In other words, peace for a week... and we can all see how that feels.

EDDIE (CONT'D)

And I'm _in_ as far as that goes, peace and any chance to stay in bed for a week, count me in. If everybody had to stay in bed except pizza delivery guys, that'd be perfect. So there he is, in bed with his wife, Yoko Ono. He's got the beard, the long hair, pajamas. She's got her bathrobe on. That's in bed for a week without cable– that's heavy. They're just singing songs and making signs, "Hair peace"... "Bed peace"... "Give peace a chance." I love John Lennon. He was beautiful... John Lennon, heavy Beatle. Paul McCartney, light Beatle. George Harrison, quiet Beatle. Ringo Starr, right place at the right time. That guy got the best job in history of jobs. He walked right in. Say _I_ lived in Liverpool, late 50s early 60s,– knew how to play drums– came by, said hello to everybody, got along. It could be John, Paul, George and Eddie. But don't get me wrong, I like Ringo Starr. But that's a lucky guy, that guy... I got him on the jukebox. That song, Photograph...

And now the jukebox is all CD's, you could fit a lot on. And I keep up on that jukebox. I'm all over it. I got some great stuff in there. Stones, "Exile on Main Street," great album. Some Kinks, Ray Davies is a genius. Got some wild stuff like Iggy Pop, "I Wanna be Your Dog." I dig that Iggy pop, he's fucking nuts that, guy. Got some blues. Muddy Waters, Johnny Winter, Johnny "Guitar" Watson. Some jazz– Miles Davis, Dexter Gordon, John Coltrane. It's music I like. Music I enjoy. Like I say, running a bar's a lot of work; I'm here constantly. It's a tough job. But it's what I do and it's what I do best. And that's that.

So it was nice talking to you, thanks for stopping by. Come back any time. Remember "Eddie's" 97 Genesee Street, Downtown Buffalo. See ya then... thanks.

Exit.

Curtain.

Additional titles from Steele Spring Stage Rights

By BRENT HAZELTON | Play with music | 1M | 1 hour 50 minutes

"Liberace! dazzles the eyes and ears." *–Thirdcoast Digest*

Meet the man behind the grand. *Liberace!* Is a moving and highly entertaining tribute to the performer and musician famous for his charm, glitz, and glamour. On a set reminiscent of his celebrated television program, Liberace relives the highs (and lows) of his prolific life, revealing the real person behind the persona of an enormously talented and acclaimed performer in American history. Interwoven with a rollicking piano score spanning classical and popular music from Chopin to "Chopsticks," and Rachmaninoff to Ragtime, this solo-performer tour de force will have your audience cheering the life of a uniquely American icon.

by ROB LAUER

Comedy | 2F, 4M, 2 Girls, 2 Boys | 1 Hour, 45 Minutes

Lights! Camera! Prayer!

Journey back to the late 1960s on the television set of *Tom and Penny's Yard Party*: an evangelical show for children on WJIK-TV (Where Jesus Is King). Tom and Penny are a young married couple who broadcast their wholesome "Jesus loves you!" message to living rooms across the country. As the stress of off-camera station politics and the reality of their troubled marriage come to a head, Tom and Penny's world begins to unravel and we see a far less polished side to our bible-thumping hosts. When Penny reads a fan letter from the mother of an odd young boy in the studio audience, everything falls apart–live and on air. **Tune in! This dark comedy of errors is sure to make you a true believer.**

www.stagerights.com

Additional titles from Steele Spring Stage Rights

WATSON
The Last Great Tale of the Legendary
Sherlock Holmes

By JAIME ROBLEDO | Comedy | 4F, 7M | 1 hour 45 minutes

"Inventive, epic comedy." –*Los Angeles Times*

A mystery, a legend, an enduring friendship. *Watson: The Last Great Tale of the Legendary Sherlock Holmes* tells the story of a good man trapped in the shadow of a great man. Funny, moving, and theatrically inventive, this high-energy play balances witty comedy and dramatic mystery to recount the last great tale of the legendary Sherlock Holmes as seen through the eyes of his trusted friend and colleague, Dr. John H. Watson. From pantomime to *Punch and Judy* and with the theatrical ingenuity of Broadway's *The 39 Steps, Watson* tells a grand tale of heroes and villains that will captivate your audience until the very end! **"A real crowd pleaser!"** –*Backstage*

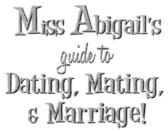

Miss Abigail's guide to Dating, Mating, & Marriage!

By KEN DAVENPORT & SARAH SALTZBERG

Comedy | 1F, 1M | 75 minutes

"PURE FUN! You can't help but fall instantly in love with Miss Abigail's Guide!" - *Entertainment Weekly*

Let Miss Abigail take you back to a simpler time, before booty calls and speed-dating, back when the divorce rate wasn't 50% and when 'fidelity' was more than an investment firm! It's *Loveline* meets *Dr. Ruth* as Miss Abigail shares her vast knowledge of every piece of relationship literature known to mankind. The audience participates in this hilarious variety show, and Miss Abigail's strapping young assistant Paco is there to provide for her every need. This smash off-Broadway hit will keep you laughing all night long – that's the Miss Abigail guarantee! **"Big laughs!"** –*Associated Press;* **"Truly a Can't Miss!"** –*Harper's Bazaar*

www.stagerights.com

By VICTOR L. CAHN

Drama | 3F | 80 minutes

A Gripping Political Thriller

Charlotte runs an influential political blog from her home on Cape Cod. Irene, working for a long-time Senator in the midst of a tough campaign, supplies Charlotte with damaging material about the Senator's opponent. Megan, an aide to that opponent, arrives with new reports, and the three power-brokers lock horns in a battle of manipulation and political intrigue. As charges escalate and the battle swerves in unexpected directions, these highly intelligent and articulate women serve up blackmail, power plays, and plenty of media spin. In other words, politics as usual! **"A tight drama, cleverly constructed!"** –*New York Theatre Wire*

by DON GOODRUM

Based on the classic story by Stephen Vincent Benet

Drama | 1F, 5M, Ensemble | 2 hours

A Classic Tale That Proves There Is No Such Thing As A Free Lunch

The devil is known by many names, but we all know that he's not to be trusted, even in one's darkest hour. Jabez, a poor soul who can't seem to catch a break, has hit his personal low when a man named Scratch shows up to offer a deal; seven years of prosperity in exchange for his soul. Jabez takes the deal and his life takes a miraculous turn for the better, that is until it comes time to pay the piper. Now, with his eternal soul hanging in the balance, he hires famed lawyer Daniel Webster to get him out of a contract straight from hell. In a tale that draws as much from an episode of *Law and Order* as it does from history, this is the fight of the century, and one man's life and the future of a nation are at stake. **"A clever re-telling. Charming on every level!"** –Northwest Florida Daily News

www.stagerights.com

Additional titles from Steele Spring Stage Rights

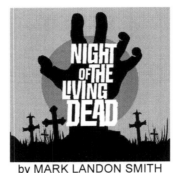

by MARK LANDON SMITH
Comedy | 4F, 4M, Ensemble | 60 Minutes
The Original Zombie Movie Comes Back To Life On Stage!

Run! Hide! Lock the doors! After a NASA probe contaminated with mysterious radiation crashes to Earth, the recently deceased begin to rise again, and boy are they hungry! They may be out to eat the living, but these walking dead are rampant with wit and sarcasm—certainly a breed above your garden-variety carnivores. Based on the cult classic film by George A. Romero, this zombie-thon is a delightfully skewed send-up of one of the most beloved science fiction genres of all time. Fast-paced and packed with contagious humor, you'll laugh yourself to death over these horrifically and hysterically misunderstood flesh-eating monsters. Dedicated to the zombie in all of us. **These Living Dead Will Leave You In Stitches!**

By BETH KANDER
Comedy | 3F, 3M | 90 Minutes
Political Scandal, Family Style

Sam Storm has been the beloved mayor of Anderson, Georgia for the past twenty years. Loved by the community and his doting wife, Sam's name is usually the only one on the ballot come election time, but when an embarrassing video of him is leaked his seat in office is threatened. Sam has some real competition when the last person he ever expected to run against him puts her name on the ballot, his wife Sophia. Now it's down and dirty as husband and wife duke it out. Can their marriage withstand the political fisticuffs? And what happens when an unexpected third candidate enters the race? This fast-paced political comedy brings new meaning to the phrase "family politics." **A bright new comedy from the creator of "Scrambled" and "See Jane Quit"**

www.stagerights.com

Additional titles from Steele Spring Stage Rights

Music and Lyrics by RYAN SCOTT OLIVER
Book by KIRSTEN GUENTHER
Musical | 3F, 2M | 70 minutes

"Sophisticated and impressively clever." –*LAist*

Out Of My Head is a compelling new musical from Ryan Scott Oliver, recipient of the American Theatre Wing's Jonathan Larson Grant and the prestigious Richard Rodgers Award for Musical Theatre. Five 20-something strangers bare their hearts and souls as they journey through their lives, loves, and losses during a pair of free group therapy sessions. From the moment of their breakdowns to their ultimate breakthroughs, the smart and emotional interplay of these quirky characters brings them all the self-discovery to set aside their insecurities and face the world anew— a little less frightened and a little more brave than before. This fresh and contemporary chamber musical celebrates the amazing strength of the human spirit. **"Witty and provocative."** –*Backstage*

By BETH KANDER | Comedy | 3F, 2M | 95 minutes

"A raucous new comedy!" –*Jackson Free Press*

Jane's life turns upside down on the worst possible day: the day she decides to quit smoking! When this 30-year old waitress announces to her friends and family that she's quitting "for real," they're supportive. In fact, they're a little bit too supportive. Each has n explosive announcement of their own to share, from a looming divorce to an impending sexual crisis, but nobody wants to be responsible for Jane falling off the non-smoking wagon. As they trip over themselves to keep their secrets secret, who would suspect that Jane is keeping the biggest secret of all? Will Jane quit quitting? This delightful southern comedy proves that you can quit smoking, but you can't quit your crazy family! **"Light-hearted and entertaining—a playful Southern romp!"** –*Lexington Herald Leader*

www.stagerights.com

By PERRY STEELE PATTON | Comedy | 3F, 2M | 2 hours

A profoundly moving comedy with southern charm.

Former beauty queen Ima Jean Walker returns to her hometown after a twenty-year absence, self-assured of winning a local contest she believes will jump-start her long-delayed country music career. Tempers flare and southern sparks fly when her famous high school rival appears in a whirlwind and upsets Ima Jean's unfulfilled dreams of stardom. *A Breath of Dusty Air* is a touching story of loss, longing, and never forgotten dreams, reminding us that voices from our past never fade away, but return to whisper of journeys long since forgotten.

Created by C. STEPHEN FOSTER, CHUCK PELLETIER, and ROD DAMER

Musical | 2F, 2M | 90 minutes

"A bright musical with breezy wit and irony." *–Los Angeles Times*

John, Cliff, Anna, and Divonne live out their complicated lives in the green room of their school's theatre department. Both hilarious and heartwarming, this modern musical gives an authentic account of the struggles these four college theatre majors have in finding their place in the world. The rock-infused pop score includes the Songwriter's Guild of America award-winning song, "It's All About Me." If you've ever been an actor or wanted to be an actor, you'll certainly relate to the Broadway dreams of these characters in this sure-fire hit! **"A surprisingly sweet tale of ambition and talent."** *–Sacramento Bee*

www.stagerights.com

Made in the USA
Charleston, SC
12 June 2015